Picasso's
— Piebald —
Perspectives

(...the pony, that is, not the artist)

Ruth Whittaker

Grosvenor House
Publishing Limited

This book is published by
Grosvenor House Publishing Ltd
Link House
140 The Broadway, Tolworth, Surrey, KT6 7HT.
www.grosvenorhousepublishing.co.uk

This book is a work of fiction although the story
is based on real creatures, people and events.

A CIP record for this book
is available from the British Library

ISBN 978-1-80381-301-1

To John, for buying Picasso for me.

Contents

Foreword

Those of us who share our lives with beings of another species will most likely have, at times, speculated on what is passing through the minds of our companions. What are they 'thinking'?

This delightful collection of writing, makes a valiant attempt to answer this question. Replete with sardonic humour and keen observation, it documents a never-ending tug-o-war between two equally determined protagonists. Who is going bend their will to accommodate the other in the pursuit of daily tasks and rituals? Who will cede? Who will vanquish? Everyday routines of feeding, grooming, cleaning, watering and riding offer huge scope for comedic interpretation. Daily vicissitudes and modest triumphs and reconciliations are mined for our amusement, edification and delight.

Inter-species communications, especially that enjoyed in the company of domesticated animals, introduces enormous capacity for misunderstanding, and the very fact of our proximity amplifies this risk. Our elected affinity ushers in the infinite subtlety of nuance and speculation in the absence of a shared, precise, language. It is the writer's self-deprecating speculations that inject these episodic accounts with hilarity, respect and humility. In turn, it is the disdainful hubris of Picasso that reigns supreme in these tales of encounter and exchange. Nevertheless she, for Picasso is a 'she', calculatedly recognises the benefits of a working symbiotic relationship. A treat goes a long way to mollify and ameliorate.....

It is this gradually emergent symbiosis and mutual, albeit grudging, affection that make this collection of episodic anecdotes so absorbing. The writing style is immensely accessible and assured. It articulates the battle of will in terms that would be as inviting to children, especially lovers of ponies, as to adults who will be familiar with relationships where bickering pervades.

One of the many aspects of the writing that greatly appeals is the equality between the species, between the two equally matched forces, that is established at the outset. Each is accorded respect as 'beings' existing on the same horizon, lying outwith misplaced notions of hierarchy. It is this predetermined equality, the even plane, that allows for the amusingly stubborn determination from both the two and four-legged version to emerge. These finely wrought, keenly observed, often curmudgeonly exchanges offer up observations that truly tickle and enhance. Enhancement comes in the form of the insights generated through small incremental shifts in rapport that reward the reader attuned to this register of exchange.

Jim Mooney 2022

Professor Jim Mooney, Scottish-born artist, teacher and writer, holds several Visiting Professorships in Art, and is a Fellow of the Royal College of Art. He divides his time between his homes in London and Portgower, on the East Coast of Sutherland.

Preface

You don't need to be an art-lover, or horse-lover, to read this. It's about everyday life seen through the sardonic, non-matching eyes of Willows Picasso, a black and white Gypsy Cob pony mare, whose two-leg I am.

Picasso IS female, to be clear. I didn't choose her name, and as it's considered bad form to change it, I haven't. Yes, her eyes don't match. That on her right is normal horsey dark blueish brown, while her left is disconcertingly azure. No-one's perfect. Nonetheless, Picasso's baleful gaze misses very little, from the ineptitude of her enthusiastic if decrepit two-leg (still nursing distant memories of nerveless pony-mad teens) to the approach of titbits.

Acknowledgments

Ailsa Skirving-Carrick , the only girl I know who wasn't terrified of our irascible art teacher at Jordanhill College School, for the final picture.

Amie Macdonald (Amie's Clipping & Grooming) for much equine depilation

Anne White, saddle fitter

Becky Dickie, my daughter, for sourcing Picasso in the first place

Diane Mackay, Doll Riding Centre, for instruction and guidance through UHI Level 6

Kessock Equine Vets, for filing teeth, vaccinations, wormers and the odd invoice.

Linda Gill for the front cover illustration and unfailing friendship.

Lorna Jappy, my neighbour, for always coaxing Picasso into the horsebox

Lucy and Tommy, Shore Garage Helmsdale, for keeping the horsebox on the road

Natalie Vincent, Pottofields Equestrian Centre, for breaking in Picasso

Nicole Hawker, farrier, for trimming Picasso's hooves regularly

Stephen Cruickshank, for two useful lessons

1. I arrive

Picasso here. Someone told HER they wanted to know more about me. Shows their good taste, so here goes.

The illustration above clearly marks the most significant moment in a two-leg's life, i.e., when one of US is delivered safely into it. This was how, many winter coats ago, I was offloaded onto HER... What would you call it? SHE undeniably and embarrassingly cares for me, but... SHE wasn't what I was used to.

Previously:

Was dragged away from my mum. Actually, beyond nipping me and telling me to mind my manners, Mum'd long abandoned me for the boy in the next field.

Next. Trundled away in various moving boxes, till I spent a very pleasant time with Natalie. Here I was put through my paces, and sussing that this was a good berth, did my best to impress. Really liked Natalie, and followed her around, even after she'd jumped down off my back, keen to emphasise my loyalty. Failed. Was loaded into a trailer, and trundled somewhere else.

Epic fail. New two-legs slung their nearest saddle-thing on to my back, swiftly topping-up with another two-leg. You have no idea how agonising it was! I did the only sensible thing, and bucked the agony right off again. After several action replays, I'd generated much upset, but the plonkers were too plonkerish to realise that their Jurassic saddle was too long for my back. How would they have liked someone sitting heavily on their sensitive kidneys? Anyway, result! Natalie took me back, but sadly only for a short time, before one of those vet know-alls looked me over and under, and before you could say 'walk on', I was walked away from Natalie, and onto another box.

Had to endure some time in the company of a snivelling kid, all the way from Natalie's to... Who knew where? Sprog kept grizzling for her mum, till I told her to shut it, or I'd bite her, which did the trick, though I couldn't actually reach through. Finally, a he-two-leg let me out (I won't pretend I wasn't a tad anxious by then) and handed me over to HER - the silly old biddy, sporting a most unfortunate hat. To be quite fair, SHE immediately gave me personally-bitten-off chunks of apple, then led me up to a new field, where SHE took off my halter, allowing me to have a look around, and a relaxing roll. The box thing drove away, taking the grizzling youngster with it, thank goodness. I'd have bullied it 24/7, just because I could.

The bad-hatted SHE wobbled off eventually, after showing me where nice clean water was. Over the fence were two girls, one small and black, the other tall, elegant and chestnut. We all said hello, then...

"If you try my grass, I'll kick you," said the little one.

"If you try my grass, I'll bite you," said the tall one.

Usual friendly introductions. Thoroughly savvy, I responded as etiquette demands. "If you even

3

think of trying *my* grass, I'll lame the hoofing pair of you."

It's always nice to be nice, and from that moment, we were on the best of terms.

That was the beginning of the middle of the end of my first day with HER.

To be continued. Oh yes.

2. I am trimmed and saddled

Another memorable morning for HER began as her offspring collected me from my new field.

"Come on, Picasso!"

I was wary, as only the morning after arriving, I was led off to see a two-leg called Nicole who insisted on picking up my hooves, and trimming bits off them. It didn't hurt, but wariness pays when in completely new surroundings, and I snorted a little, just to advise her of my potential, if necessary.

Anyway, I allowed the offspring to catch me (a carrot was involved) and lead me to yet another new location. There SHE was, with yet another two-leg – Anne – whom I was destined to meet quite often thereafter. The purpose of this, I sussed, was to fit me up with the saddle thing two-legs sit on. I have concluded that two-legs couldn't manage to ride us without one.

After trying several types, a suitable model was selected, and strapped firmly around my neat flanks.

"Will she blow up?" asked Anne.

"I don't know..." SHE quavered.

"Come on, Mum!" encouraged the offspring.

I was both embarrassed and disgusted to be led to a nearby wall, and held by one, while the other coaxed HER to fling a leg across my back. To my relief, SHE got aboard quite gently, but I knew that SHE was anxious. One of them led me around, while SHE began to get the feel of things. SHE was given some much-needed reminders, such as not clutching my reins so tightly, if SHE wanted me to move off. I was in deep despair, actually starting to think about putting on a performance, to serve the silly old thing right for being so yellow, reflecting, however, that I'd have to put my back into dislodging HER solid carcass. SHE prodded me feebly with her heels, and after ambling around HER back field, we walked down to the road, where, to my relief, SHE urged me into a trot. We successfully travelled a short distance and back again, to loud acclaim from HER supporters. SHE lavished lots of fawning praise and carrots on me, before HER offspring removed my new equipment, and returned me to my own field.

I needed to evaluate. It seemed that although pathetically nervous, SHE did seem to know more or less what to do, once on my back, and SHE was kindly. I just hoped that I might have a bit more fun, but told myself that it was early days.

"What happened?" asked the snooty chestnut girl across the fence. "Did you win that round?"

"I was chosen by HER, because I'm super reliable, unlike you, I imagine."

Turning my back, I lifted my tail, and deposited a satisfactory heap of poop as close to her as I could. I *am* reliable.

3. My neurotic companion

Picasso's pal? Perhaps that's too effusive, with more than a chime of insincerity? Yes. I allow this fellow creature to share my amenities, and thus enjoy advantages she'd never otherwise have, but don't consider us close. The name by which she's known is Vala.

To begin with, SHE hollered hopelessly, as my new companion (NC) ignored her. Tired of the hopeless hollering, I threatened a nip, encouraging NC to amble over.

"SHE's calling you," I pointed out, coldly.

"Who? Where? Why? Am I going to die?"

You'll gather that my NC is hopelessly neurotic, always looking on the black side of things.

"SHE is calling you - can't you hear HER? SHE's calling your name - Vala!"

"That's not my name! That's *not* my name!"

Much snorting and eye-rolling, but unimpressed, I continued. "Buck up - no, not literally, you idiot! Hurry over and see what SHE wants! Oh, please yourself!" Exasperated, I plodded leisurely over to HER, collecting a tasty morsel that ought to have gone to Vala, who'd followed me at a tentative distance.

9

"See?" I said, through a crunchy mouthful. "This is what SHE's usually about."

SHE continued to make HER range of silly noises in Vala's direction, until the equally silly brute stretched her silly neck far enough to take the treat with the tips of her lips.

"It's poisonous," I commented, for fun.

Vala sprang backwards, then paused, savouring the goody.

"You're quite the stupidest beast I've ever met," I remarked pleasantly. I like to give a warm welcome to visitors – she's the third since I've been here.

By this stage, Vala was actually shaking, and SHE had to advance very slowly before being able to grasp the thing round her head.

"What's going to happen to me? Will SHE hurt me?"

You'd hardly believe that she was breaking out in a sweat. I only sweat when a very determined two-leg makes me do something effortful.

"No, but I'm going to." I moved in for a quick teasing nip, but, to my astonishment, Vala turned her heels at me in a flash, and I had to take prompt evasive action. Assessing the situation, I acknowledged that Vala was a little bit bigger than me, and although she hadn't previously showed me her hooves or teeth,

I instantly took the point that she was a skilled operator, and withdrew to a safe distance. Violence isn't my thing. Neither is bullying, of course.

SHE, in the meantime, maintained HER soundtrack of soothing sounds, and produced something else from the place where SHE stores the treats.

"I'm for it now!" snorted Vala. "SHE's going to hurt me! I'll die! I'll... Oh, that was nice..."

Undeterred by these hysterics, SHE had gently spread some interesting-smelling stuff on Vala's muzzle, and below her eye. Next, SHE moved to Vala's shoulder, then her hind leg. I watched closely, and realised that all the areas SHE was anointing were very sore, for some reason.

"Oh, that's better! That's much better! Thank you, My Person!"

SHE put HER stuff away, but Vala didn't budge, standing beside HER, oozing pathetic gratitude. Unable to endure such a loser attitude, I decided to lighten things up.

"C'mon! Now SHE's finished foozling around with you, let's have some fun! I'll show you how to sneak up and nudge HER into a poop pile!"

Vala looked at me. She really was bigger than me. I gave a little stamp, to encourage her, but then she

11

replied, "You ill-mannered little piece of dung that you are! If you even think of harming HER - MY two-leg - I'll batter you so soft that it's straight they'll be pouring you into cans of dog food!"

You may imagine how taken aback I was. Never had one of my kind spoken to me like that. I decided to ignore her uncouth response, and sidled towards her, intent on having the last laugh. Vala lashed out, making me shriek with surprise and pain, as she struck high up my quarters.

"Will you be listening to me now?"

Loud and clear. Of course, Vala's a neurotic basket case from goodness knows where. In view of her various issues, I make considerable allowances for her threatening behaviour, where SHE, or food, is concerned. I could easily put her in her place, but I'm not, as I said, a bully.

4. Pastures new

I'm picnicking daintily, while my companion wrenches the herbage up by its very roots, in her incessant quest to gorge.

Very pleasant change in the weather, thank goodness, and the day's been made absolutely perfect by moving in here, with decent grass again.

I hadn't realised that all HER fussing over the last couple of days would lead to this. Endless chugging around with that red conveyance loaded with fence posts, struggling to hitch up our water dispenser, making short, incomprehensible noises all the while. Great spectator sport. SHE's most entertaining. My companion, Vala, works herself up something chronic over HER. No idea why – I wouldn't work myself up about anything except my food, though only if I thought someone was about to pinch it, you understand. I'm not a glutton. Anyway, every time SHE let out a loud comment, Vala scurried to the gate, snorting, "SHE's hurt! SHE'll die!" in that abysmal loser way she has. I long to give her a nip. One day, I just might... Maybe.

So, after even more fiddle-faddling, SHE strode determinedly into our field, in a reasonable imitation

13

of total confidence, brandishing an enticingly-scented treat, which I thoroughly enjoyed whilst SHE applied one of the items SHE fastens around my head. SHE led me out and tied me up, leaving me to trim some stray grasses, and returned for Vala, who had already begun to hyperventilate at my removal. I didn't quite grasp the game plan to begin with, and tried to continue my trimming. Vala immediately started to chivvy. "You've got to come on, now! SHE wants us to go together with HER! If you don't, SHE'll be torn in two, then SHE'll die, then..."

"Oh, settle, petal. I'm coming," I grunted, seeing Vala's eyes rolling in that unintelligent way. So I followed at as much of a distance as I could, until, surprisingly, SHE said something rather firmly, which spurred me to quicken from crawl to plod.

I could sense that SHE was nervous, (probably 'cos SHE'd never led both of us together) for SHE kept alternately making soothing noises at Vala, and slightly stick-and-carrot noises at me. There's always a good outcome, however, when SHE's survived yet another of HER anxiety bouts, and today yielded some rather good new bite-sized munches. We had a slight moment when a car came up the hill towards us, but stood sensibly till it reversed, allowing HER to lead us into this fence-to-fence diner. SHE slipped and almost fell, which upset Vala again, and nearly jolted my neck out of joint, not that any one of you cares, but finally decanted us safely, removing our headgear and closing the gate. Blessed if I know why SHE bothered with the hassle of doing THAT. Did SHE think we were going to run away from lunch? SHE's touchingly simple.

5.   A paraphernalia

Pity me, poor Picasso that I am. What a paraphernalia of rings and buckles I had to wear. I was beyond disgusted, on several counts.

To begin with, SHE rocked up as if about to take me for an outing. I was quite pleased, as this field's expended its interest for me. So, SHE hauls me out, getting HERSELF into a fankle trying to keep Vala in, though finally settling us on our respective sides of the fence.

After howking rather a lot of squashed grass/poop mix from my hooves, and giving me an extremely superficial brushing, SHE introduced me to a new piece of kit. Momentarily, I thought, it was the heavy thing SHE lays on my back preparatory to clambering aboard, and generally struggles to fasten firmly. Natch, I do everything possible to make this awkward (sucking surreptitious air's a tried and tested ploy) but no, this was a soft thing that went all round me, and wasn't heavy. SHE tightened it up before I could work out how to obstruct. 'Vantage HER.

Next came a weird contrivance around my head. I couldn't say that it was uncomfortable, but nonetheless irksome. Thus bedecked, SHE led me to the next field down the road, while Vala wailed her usual lamentations.

"SHE'll be hurt, then SHE'll die...!"

I ignored her. Only sensible thing to do.

In the fresh field, SHE swapped my rope for a much longer version, and produced a long stick. I was unconcerned, as SHE always carries a stick of some sort, but never applies it to me. In response to HER request, I walked over to a flat-ish area, then, suddenly, remembered what this was all about! In a dismaying flash of total recall, hours spent literally going round in circles under the variously gruelling regimes of Natalie, Anne and HER offspring came back to me. Shaking my head to clear my thoughts, I comforted myself that SHE is by no means from the same stable, so to speak, and felt a glimmer of hope ignite. I allowed HER to fumble around with HER long rein and useless stick, till SHE instructed me to, "Walk on!"

Walk, my hoof! Trot, my hoof! Decided to scare the living daylights out of HER, by imitating a much bigger boy I once saw, who set off galloping round at full tilt. Annoyingly, SHE didn't react as planned – you know, letting me go – so I just had to keep thundering round. Heard HER muttering something Diane said, about not letting the rope touch the ground, as SHE tried not to truss HERSELF up.

I perceived that, fortunately, SHE was tiring, so gradually slackened the old pace to a confrontational sort of trot, sensing that a titbit wouldn't be far away. SHE's so predictable. I came to a standstill, allowing HER to drench me in praise, and accepted a munchable. All done? Oh dear me, no. Next thing, SHE fiddles around with the long rope and that pretentious stick, and sent me off going t'other way around! I attempted the I'm-going-to-run-you-down gambit, but quite unexpectedly, SHE trundled HERSELF out of the way, and tapped that blasted stick on the ground behind my heels, leaving me no option other than cracking on once more. This time it was highly unpleasant. I don't much mind going round *that* way, but I hate going round *this* way. I couldn't decide the best course of action, and losing my habitual cool, started to lower my head and kick up my heels between strides. This, I have to admit, produces rather unladylike results for those employing the air-sucking girth-obstructing tactic, slightly diminishing overall intimidation effects.

All things must end, however, and gratifyingly soon, SHE reeled me in, stoked up my titbit level, and returned me, sweating slightly, I confess, to my field. Nothing compared to HER, who had to shed HER hat, gloves and jacket before feeling cool enough to pick our poop. Hope SHE gets the message. Enough's enough.

6. Primped up

Primped up Picasso. Whatever next? Bothering no one, when SHE hauls me away from my field and ties me up, admittedly with a hay net for company. Next, SHE starts scrabbling about with my mane – pleased to report it wasn't going well, judging by all those cross words SHE was mumbling through a mouthful of hairbands. Silly old boiler. Then, SHE staggers round to my tail to attempt something similar. Yes, I could've easily kicked HER, but I'm not that

stupid – who'd take over from HER, eh? Someone with more of a clue about how to work me harder? Not worth it. Hope to goodness this Diane SHE keeps referring to, lets HER pass whatever test this inconvenience represents.

7. Practical Picasso

Practical Picasso takes charge.

Yes indeed, my useless neurotic companion was in habitual meltdown, because SHE was sitting snivelling beside HER trolley jack and our water bowser. I, of course, keeping my head when all around are losing theirs, was sensibly nosing around in the back of the quad for what SHE'd lost.

The morning began normally enough, HER piloting HER noisy quad into the field, with a view to collecting our water bowser, and taking it away to refill. I love it when SHE brings this mechanical steed, and make a point of jostling it, and generally getting in the way. SHE always struggles to hook up the bowser, so I infallibly offer loads of moral support – breathing down HER neck, testing HER pocket for treats – you know the sort of thing. Finally, SHE remounted and rode away. For once, SHE'd devised an exit strategy that thwarted my plan to follow, but there was compensation, as things would rapidly enliven.

As we watched HER towing purposefully uphill, the water bowser suddenly broke free and bolted backwards, putting in a buck which turned it more or less upside down, leaving it high and, well, dry, in the road. SHE didn't notice immediately, then drove back and dismounted.

Vala's hysteria was predictable.

"That thing is dangerous! SHE'll be..."

"Killed. Very likely." I've sussed that it's best to truncate Vala's lamentations before she works up a real head of steam. We watched as SHE struggled in vain to right our bowser, only managing to manoeuvre it to the road side. Some time elapsed, then Lucy (whom I enjoy being ridden by, from time to time) arrived with reinforcements, and, thanks to this, after some toing and froing, SHE was able to resume the fill-up mission. All prime spectator sport stuff.

SHE returned at last, crawling cravenly, followed by the full bowser. Remembering how it had bolted earlier, I decided not to jostle it, but looked on as SHE came to a standstill at the correct place. Once certain of its immobility, I ambled over, to cheer HER on again, admiring HER persistence in replacing the concrete chocks I so relish rubbing out of place, once HER back's turned. With much puffing and panting (total attention-seeking) SHE rammed HER heavy trolley jack under the tow bar (I know these names because I've heard HER murderous moans about their various shortcomings, so often) then exhibited pathetic despair. I nosed about in the back of the quad, because that's what SHE does, and this prompted HER to rootle and find whatever it was SHE needed to raise the bowser free of the quad. I was quite exhausted by HER emotional backwash, and frankly disappointed that, after all that, SHE forgot to give me a titbit.

8.   Event alert

"Pi-ca-sso!"

Event alert. SHE jolted in on her four-wheeled thing, armed with all sorts of kit, but, significantly, a veritable barrel of carrots. Never one to pass over additional nourishment, I allowed HER to fasten whatever it is round my head, while accepting my rightful crunchy tribute. SHE didn't then lead me out and apply the usual we're-going-for-a-nice-jog protocols, instead giving me an absentminded sort of pat, before turning HER attention to my companion, who's actually as companionable as a tick in the muzzle.

Before my companion remembered to escape, SHE pressed a fistful of carrots on her, deftly applying the head-thing. "Not so smart at giving the slip these days - you're getting too old!" I remarked, conversationally. Truth never hurts. My companion merely rolled her eyes malevolently, intent on her carrot. You wouldn't believe her affectation. She takes titbits gently from HER, chewing them very slowly and carefully. I, on the other hand, grab offerings as soon as they appear (once had to spit out some paper covering) and hoover them down

ASAP, in order to maximise intake. I'm not in the least bit greedy, merely businesslike.

SHE shuffled away back to HER transport, and sat there, staring at a sheaf of coloured papers for a while (two-legs are endlessly odd) until another two-leg arrived in a large white conveyance. They communicated in the quaint way they have - never understand why, especially if they don't seem to be acquainted, one doesn't bite/kick the other, to demonstrate superiority? More carrots later, SHE led me out beyond that nasty fence that smacks if you touch it, failing as ever to prevent me from dropping my head to munch. It was product plus to hear HER being rebuked for this, by the other two-leg, and hilarious to resist HER feeble attempts to pull my head up again. I only obliged so's not to miss the next instalment of carrot from HER bulging side pannier. The other two-leg became even more irritated, and it was diverting to feel HER torn between apprehension of one or the other of us.

An unexpected little jab in my upper shoulder area was a surprise, but was over as soon as I noticed it, enabling me to refocus on hassling HER.

You'll find this hard to believe, but somehow I began not care about those carrots, nor that the visiting two-leg rested my head on a ledge of some sort, hauled open my mouth, propped it wide with a cold hard object, and selfishly removed much of the half-chewed carrot I'd squirrelled away for later. I cared even less that this creature started excavating deep into my head with something that sounded like HER transport, and not in the least that SHE was stroking me gently (which I normally detest) making that strange sound pattern with HER voice, which is interesting, up to a point.

The sun warmed my back. From some dozy distance, my companion fretted that I was probably going to die, but standing there, I knew, because I could scent concealed carrots, that everything was very good indeed. SHE led me back after the other had finished messing about, and I only just remembered to encourage my companion - "It's awful - you'll hate it!" - before simply having to lock my knee joints and have another little zizz.

9.   I am totally stressed

I am totally stressed, and almost unable to touch my hay. Just joking.

It's been a stimulating time for your long-suffering Picasso, with last week's visiting two-leg sticking needles in me, and mining the private recesses of my mouth, accompanied by the default position panics of my companion and HER.

This morning, before the sun was properly up, SHE rolled in, oozing that brand of jollity which, I've come to recognise, inevitably heralds an out-of-the-ordinary event which will worry HER much more than me. We duly trotted up, intrigued by the enticing scent of something SHE held out to us. I let my companion go first. There's sound sense in this, firstly because my companion is turbo-prompt with the heels-threat, but also because once she gets her chompers into something, it takes her a ridiculous time to process it, thus leaving the field clear for me to clean up. The offering was small but very pleasant. I disposed of it, disappointed that there was no more. SHE took HERSELF off for a short time, returning to footer about, as ever. Then, two more two-legs arrived. I recognised them as Nicole and

Nick, who pick up my feet, rasp away at them, and recently, rivet on those hard things that make such a noise on the road.

SHE attempted to catch my companion, who actually disgraced both HER and me, by running away, bleating as usual, about being killed. Moving to Plan B, SHE produced a fat bucketful of inducement, which you may suppose isn't something I ever need to be asked about twice. SHE held firmly onto my rope – what nonsense! I could escape HER anytime, though why would I, where food's concerned? The Nick set about my feet, and to my disappointment, did whatever he did before I'd munched even halfway down the bucket, which was then removed, along with my rope.

I watched amused, as my companion was lured into being caught.

"I'm frightened of him!" she snorted, nostrils flaring.

"Probably eats nutters like you!" I agreed, just to stir things up.

Finally, SHE convinced my craven companion that it was safe for her to sample the bucket. To my annoyance, Nicole, 500% more us-savvy than HER, moved my companion and the bucket beyond the fence, and therefore beyond my reach, while her feet were attended to.

For whatever reason, SHE's decided to remove our hard foot-coverings. I also wanted to know why, when SHE resumed the daily poop-pick, SHE hadn't brought more titbits. I was quite cross, especially after the bucket deprivation, and jostled HER on HER way, trying to give HER sleeve a reproachful nip. SHE made an ungrateful sort of noise, which immediately brought my companion over at top speed. I won't repeat the name she called me, as I scuttled to dodge her hostile heels. Almost as offensive, was the way SHE and my companion then had one of their little love-ins, complete with much poll-scratching and nauseating swearing of eternal loyalty. You'll never accuse me of either swearing or loyalty.

10. Was it something I did?

Apparently, HER grand offspring has transferred her affections from me, Picasso, to Another. I won't pretend I'm not disgruntled. Was it something I did?

Last time the grand-offspring had the privilege of sitting on me, we had a walk around the locality, her sibling aboard my companion. My companion hurries everything, from the acquisitive, frankly greedy, way she bolts any nutrition heading in her direction, to her irritating inability to stroll in a leisurely manner.

We were as I related, strolling, my companion, however, drawing further and further ahead. I couldn't have cared less, enabled as I was to snatch surreptitious mouthfuls of fresh greenstuffs, as I ambled. Suddenly, my paranoid companion, imagining that she was effectively alone on a hostile track lined with predatory sheep, began to hyperventilate, calling pathetically for my help. Intrinsically caring, I grudgingly raised my head, and actioned some speed to catch up with her, while carefully retaining my latest mouthful. Unfortunately, my change of mode was misinterpreted by the grand-offspring, who promptly emitted distressed noises, attracting much fuss from her dam and HER. I stopped immediately, having caught up, and earned a great deal of abuse from my companion for having frightened my passenger. It was doubly unfair, because I'd only been trying to soothe my companion, and also because the grand-offspring being so lightweight, I'd quite forgotten that she was aboard - unlike HER.

This is the only possible explanation for such disloyalty from the grand-offspring.

11.   Pleasantly surprised

Pleasantly surprised Picasso, this morning.

Yesterday, SHE rolled down on that noisy red thing, laden with an assortment of objects. After SHE'd fed us and picked up our poop, SHE applied HERSELF to lugging pieces of dead trees into our field, with much puffing and panting.

I watched with great interest (my companion habitually distressing herself over what might happen) as SHE set two pieces together then became upset as they fell apart again. After several attempts, SHE seemed to have stuck them together, and quickly added another couple of pieces. It began to drizzle, and SHE departed on the noisy thing.

This morning, SHE returned on her own hooves, and while we ate our feed, (if you can call what my companion does 'eating', i.e., thrusting her greedy muzzle into her bowl, scattering its contents far and wide) SHE did some more work on the dead tree structure, and began to shove it towards us. Judging by HER return to puffing and panting (like my companion tackling a hill) it was a tough task, and feeling sorry for HER, we flanked HER as

SHE pushed and tugged the thing to where SHE wanted it to be.

Next, SHE threw a little hay out to where we feed, which absorbed mega-muncher's attention to the exclusion of all else. Because there was no point in even trying to pull out a couple of wisps for myself, I watched for HER next move. See how my generosity towards my greedy companion was rewarded! SHE now toted a huge wedge of hay, which SHE tipped into the heavy thing. Immediately, I grasped the situation, and tucked happily into the new hay-dispenser, while Dobbin Dimwit continued to pick at the wisps on the ground. Sooner or later, guzzler will get the message, but until then? Make hay while the sun shines!

12. Pathetically pleading

Pathetically pleading Picasso. Unlike me, I know, but I'd had a bad morning. Of course, it was wet and windy which we don't like, yet no excuse for that co-creature's behaviour towards me.

SHE arrived, bringing breakfast, and I was glad SHE couldn't totally understand that my companion was actually telling HER to hurry up! Disgracefully greedy. As usual, SHE set about refilling our water, before distributing our feeds. The eating machine, unable to wait a moment longer, rudely pawed the ground - too dense to realise that this just makes it muddy. Anyway, SHE placed her food in front of her, while I waited at a distance for mine. Not content with simply shovelling into her own bowl, however, she suddenly turned her heels on me, as I cautiously picked my way to mine. Taken by surprise, I lost my footing on the slippery slope, almost fell, and cried out from the pain of the kick, and the wrench to one of my legs.

"That'll show you! Think you're the surefooted one?" my companion sneered unpleasantly into my feed.

It was SO unfair, not least because I *am* very surefooted indeed, which donkey-features certainly isn't, but also because I hadn't been bothering her at all. You will appreciate how upset I was, as I couldn't even face my feed.

SHE, however, showed a side I've never seen before, and seizing the thing SHE picks our poop with, SHE brandished it threateningly at my bullying companion, and used HER voice in a horrible loud way I've never heard before. I knew perfectly well that SHE wasn't actually going to hit her, but you should've seen my companion retreat, eyes rolling wildly, pleading not to be killed. Typical bully. SHE moved my feed even further away, called me over and gave me a nice soothing rub. When hay time arrived, I kept checking that SHE was ready to protect me once more, but once hay-burner's properly engaged with gorging, there's nothing to fear.

Odd, really. SHE's much smaller and feebler than we are, but today even I thought SHE was slightly scary. On the whole, I think I'll make a point of staying on HER kind side.

13. Posing

Posing. Picasso being forced to pose, to clarify.

In SHE came and fed us. While my manger-hugging companion focused on packing her muzzle in her favourite distant corner, SHE returned, making persuasive noises, discreetly displaying some enticing titbits. Things have been rather monotonous round here lately. Just mooching around, watching my munch-crazy companion gorging, and both of us practising full speed downhill emergency stops.

SHE produced the thing that goes around my head and in my mouth - generally part of my going-out stuff, but didn't follow up with the rest of the gear. SHE then encouraged me to lift my head, while SHE pointed another accessory SHE totes, at me. In a flash, I realised SHE was shaming me, trying to make me look like something other than my incomparable self. Oh yes. I remembered watching the small black female in the next field, being be-decked in a similar fashion by her two-leg, some time ago.

I can't pretend to understand why two-legs do this sort of thing. On that occasion, the small black female was forced to wear something on her head, that made her look a truncated and tubby caricature of those horrible horned creatures that often maraud in herds into our fields, stealing our grazing. These creatures are smaller than us, but very fast, and expert at jumping. We give them a wide berth, because these horns they have are dangerously sharp. Before I knew better, when I first came here, I bustled over to chivvy two of these creatures away from my grass. They turned, cool as you please, shook their horns in my direction, and snorted, "Kill!" in their ugly way. I took their point. Returning to my reminiscence, seeing the small fat black female being made to look like a slender horned killer, made me almost split my sides laughing! I took particular trouble to tell her how utterly ridiculous she looked, but she ignored me, devouring carrots as though they were endangered.

Truthfully, I felt a twinge of remorse, as I too now stood there, looking like a despondent imitation of goodness knows what. I hoped that I wasn't modelling horns, and even more desperately that none of my kind noticed my humiliation. Manger-face still ingested hay single-mindedly however, so I breathed freely once more, as SHE removed my headgear, and posted more goodies into my relieved face.

14. Puzzled Picasso

Puzzled Picasso checking in.

My two-leg is the source of my puzzlement. When yesterday's light had faded (early - it's the dark time of the year) leaving only that pale white round thing hanging in the air above, I could still see the lights of the stable SHE lives in. However, instead of going completely dark quite soon, HER lights continued to shine. My uselessly glutinous companion began to worry, predicting colic or death for HER, to which doom-mongering I've become so accustomed, that it actually amuses me.

After some time, I could hear HER voice, because it was very still, and anyway, all of us can hear a feed bucket approaching miles away. I was, as I said, puzzled, because although SHE was clearly communicating with others of HER herd, emitting fairly jolly noises, there were no other two-legs with HER. Even grass-grabber agreed that we'd not seen, heard or scented the arrival of additional two-legs. I ambled about, twitching my ears when HER noises sounded particularly merry, moving out of the immediate firing-line from time to time, as my fellow-creature's intestinal tracts rumbled ominous prophecy of imminent evacuation. Later, very much later, HER noises stopped. I heard HER let HER smelly little meat-eater out to empty himself, then finally HER lights disappeared, and all was quiet.

I'll admit that even I was relieved to see HER this morning, as usual. I had begun to wonder if all the lights and noise were portentous of impending doom. Who, I demanded to know (of myself - I'd never share serious concerns with my pessimistic pal), would bring us food, fill up our water and our hay, if SHE should fail to do so?

Seeing HER pick HER way down, carrying (vitally important) our breakfast bucket, my relief morphed to irritation that SHE should have worried me so much in the first place. I stared at HER reproachfully, as SHE placed the larger bowl before motor-muncher. Indifferent, oblivious to my feelings, SHE even attempted to fondle my forelock, which as SHE ought to know, I detest. Worse, HER breath smelled dreadful, causing me to curl my lips back above my teeth, in involuntary disgust. SHE didn't move away a moment too soon, to poop-pick.

What bizarre two-leg ritual could possibly have generated such a long and entertaining night for HER? What did SHE mean, greeting us with, "Happy New Year, girls!"

15.   Picasso prodding around?

Picasso prodding around for a few more wisps of hay? No. In fact, I was examining my two-leg's hoof.

I've been thinking a bit more about HER lately. SHE feeds us every day, which we appreciate when it's cold and tedious. It's struck me that SHE may be slightly more intelligent than SHE seems. I've worked out that SHE feeds my companion first, dumping her enormous hay ration beside her feed bowl, so's I'll have peace to enjoy my own fodder, which SHE then drops for me, far from the totally occupied eating machine. This is quite admirably bright of HER.

SHE is disadvantaged, I realise, moving around when the ground is covered with the cold white slippery stuff. I sometimes slither, but I have another three legs waiting to bear me up. If one of HER two legs goes, SHE's in trouble, and tends to fall, making a shrill noise which immediately galvanises my dim companion into lumbering over with a view to kicking me senseless for allegedly hurting HER. As a result, I've really had to reflect on, and review, my habits when in close field proximity with HER. Gone, it would seem, are the carefree days before my current companion, when I'd show off to her predecessor,

41

the smaller brown girl, my hilarious technique for shouldering HER into a poop-pile.

In the interests of stress-free feeding, therefore, I've schooled myself to walk sedately beside HER, as SHE lugs my hay net to the dead tree container I watched HER struggling to assemble some time ago. SHE has been picking HER way very gingerly indeed, and once, SHE actually clutched at my mane to save HERSELF from falling. An imposition, though I displayed laudable tolerance. My food was at stake.

16. Breakfast chez Picasso

Breakfast chez Picasso.

On my right, visualise it, is my notional companion, Vala, power-munching away. Think yourselves lucky that you can't hear her greedy processes. On my left, and you'd have to look closely, is my black-feathered friend, Chuck. That's what I call him anyway, because it's all he seems to say. He's a cheerful chappie just the same - always lands at a respectful distance, and makes polite if incomprehensible conversation whilst I eat up my feed. Because I eat tidily and intelligently, I never leave any leftovers for Chuck. We both know, nonetheless, that my official companion throws a substantial proportion of her bowlful all over the place, in her haste to fill her face. Chuck merely has to stick around, chatting away, till I've moved across to my hay, and Muncher's moved to hers, before he can hop over and help himself to a great buffet of leftovers. Everyone's a winner, really.

17.   Springtime siesta

Springtime siesta, Picasso-style.

Yes indeed, finally the ground is warm enough to encourage me to take the weight off my hooves for a bit. My companion is stretched out at her full length, doubtless exhausted by her industrial-level forage consumption. I could almost feel sorry for what her hooves have to carry were it not that she aims them at me every morning, when SHE comes to feed us.

I almost look forward to HER visits these days, and actually hope SHE'll take me out somewhere again. No other two-leg has come to see us for such a long time, and it's been even longer since SHE's bathed me, and lured me into that mobile stable, which has taken us away to exciting events involving others of my kind. I don't know why everything's gone so quiet. All I can hear are the replete rumblings of my companion's stomach.

18. Disgusted

Disgusted and disgraced. I, Picasso, am both, to the extent of hanging my head in shame behind a conveniently edible bush.

In the foreground is my mucky mucker, truly thinking she's something because she's had her legs clipped out.

SHE pulled a fast one on her, slipping on her halter while she was busy with her morning guzzle. My companion can work herself up into a ridiculous state over life-threatening events spun from her hyperactive imagination, unless – she's eating. A pack of baying carnivores could slather around her unheeded while she's troughing. I wondered what was on the day's agenda, and approved HER forethought in ensuring we didn't have an embarrassing rerun of companion-catching, as we did when the nice two-legs came to trim our hooves, recently. I pottered up co-operatively when the next two-leg arrived, recognising that it was Amie who clips and grooms. I'm perfectly groomed at all times, but Dobinette has to have her legs, and usually her mane, clipped.

Once the job had been done, the two-legs left and silence fell, broken only by the steady munching of the depilated one. My companion has a particularly obnoxious habit: once she's finished her own food, and tidied up the last stalk from my manger, she actually roots around on the earth, rather like those disgusting grunting creatures that I once lived near to. Inevitably, her muzzle becomes as grubby as a grunter's. You can picture the scene as she lumbered over to say hello to HER, showing off what she thinks is her smart spring makeover. Do you wonder that I can't bear to look?

19. Proud Picasso

Proud Picasso. Allowing the outside world to admire me, as I stepped away from winter tedium, carrying HER for her inaugural spring hack.

Back at the OK Corral, however, my companion (who normally loathes me almost as much as I loathe her) galloped up and down our field, braying forlornly about being abandoned. No such luck. Mortifying, really. As SHE and I returned (very sedately, although I'd offered to trot, just to seem obliging), Vala came thundering back up the field to greet me, soaring over the remains of an ancient dyke, as if about to take to the skies like a lumbering piebald Pegasus. The moment I was back with her, she naturally tried to barge in and steal the piece of apple SHE'd reserved for me. SHE can be very firm when it's necessary, though, and motor-muncher had to wait her turn.

How impenetrably dense my companion is. Although SHE's dished out two bonus armfuls of hay, Vala's squabbling over mine, oblivious to her own. I have much to endure.

20.   A roll in the mud

I've had a thorough Picasso-soothing roll in the mud, to offset the stresses of being ridden downhill then uphill, punctuated by only a few stretches of straight and level. My companion had nothing more arduous than a nice brushing and a couple of titbits. I did get the brush 'n' bribe, but had to sweat, literally, for it.

Initially, I was bung full of the joys, snatching tufts of nice new grass, while SHE footered with my feet, gave me a superficial grooming, and strapped me into my working gear. I retaliated, moving my rear portions out of reach every time SHE tried to launch aboard. In great good humour, I did this two or three (well maybe four of five) times. Clearly enjoying this, SHE just led me round again and again to the thing I'm supposed to stand still by, until I became irritated, giving HER a two-second window of statuesque immobility to get HERSELF on, and stop faffing. We set off at a brisk pace, and I'd have been happy to trot, but was restrained all the way down the hill, serenaded by my companion's bleak cries of desolation.

There followed a comfortable stretch of level ground, though I was rather worried by a new hole that had cropped up to threaten me. Next, we were on the up again, and on and on and on, until I was glad SHE hadn't let me trot. Finally made it back to home base, where SHE fiddled with my feet again, and rubbed me down. There is a definite sense of purpose in HER attitude, I perceive. What can SHE have in mind?

21. Perpetually empathic

Picasso. Perpetually empathic.

SHE sat on the ground (which I could have told HER was soaking wet) making distressed noises. It was all about our water supply, which SHE had been trying to refill, only the frightening snake-thing carrying the water didn't seem long enough.

SHE had made cross noises, and fetched the four-footed thing which can haul our water supply about, if required. SHE then had to mend one of its feet by forcing some air into it, though relatively unsuccessfully. Matters went from bad to worse, every silly thing that could go wrong for HER, doing so. Nonetheless, SHE managed to refill our water supply, but struggled to free HER pulling creature from the water tank, and hurt HERSELF in the process.

For once, my companion ignored the entire performance, concentrating on grass intake. I, however, was extremely concerned, sticking my nose in occasionally, to monitor progress.

At last, SHE dropped whatever SHE was holding, and sat down on the grass, as I said. I thought perhaps

SHE might have a nice soothing roll, which I enjoy after I've been forced into effortful exercise. However, SHE just sat there making those unhappy noises. One has to rally round at such times, so I stood over HER in quietly supportive understanding, until SHE wiped HER muzzle and struggled to HER feet again.

I knew my intervention was vital. How else could SHE be reminded that a piece of carrot remained in HER pocket?

22. Perfect Picasso morning

A perfect Picasso morning. Fed, watered, Chuck, my feathered friend, diligently depilating my back of loose winter coat hairs - pooping now and again in concentration, which is slightly disconcerting, I admit. Down SHE comes, armed with all accoutrements for an outing, involving me. Been rather a lot of this sort of thing, recently All, I deduce, in the name of fittening-up.

To be fair, I feel extremely fit... Until SHE arrives on my back. I've been required to restrict my pace to a walk, which is monotonous, so it's uphill, downhill, repeat ad nauseam. To be even fairer, I suspect that much of this regime is targeted at HER. I hadn't failed to notice that HER alighting process had become somewhat laboured, to the extent that I'd come to expect her toe on my rump, as an additional ejector-aid. Poor old thing, my hoof! Under the stimulus of regular outings, SHE can now usually dismount without denting my dock, though the uphill/downhill monotony continues.

Today, we climbed a long, long hill, and even I was slightly breathless by the top. SHE gave me a breather and a slice of carrot, and the clear impression that SHE'd suffered as much if not more, than I. I wanted to hurry back down, but SHE wouldn't let me – think SHE was afraid I'd fall, silly old bat that SHE is. However, at the very bottom, SHE scared me badly, by asking me to go through some water. I won't, just won't. Who knows what's in water? Snakes, very likely. SHE tried to coax me, so pretending to co-operate, I dashed round the side at the last moment, hoping SHE'd not embarrass me by falling off. Fortunately, SHE remained aloft, but gave me a lecture about being silly and not letting the side down, which I ignored, having won the tussle anyway. Back in my field, I had to give my hard-working back a good easing roll. Getting HER fit is hard work.

23. Penitent Picasso

Penitent Picasso... Well, slightly. It really wasn't my fault.

We'd been out again. SHE brought a companion two-leg along and we all made ourselves soooooo much fitter. SHE allowed me to canter up the nice grassy path after the scary water bit, because I allowed HER to make me walk through it. I kicked up my heels several times, because it was a lovely morning, and I'd snatched some green grass. SHE wasn't dislodged, because I wasn't trying to dislodge HER.

Back in the home field, SHE removed HERSELF and all heavy gear from my back, then led me back to my companion. I don't quite know why, when I did a little dance of delight, SHE made an upset sound, and ended up on the ground. My companion lined up instantaneously.

"If you've killed HER, I'll kill you," she stated flatly. No reason to doubt her.

"I haven't done anything to HER..." I began, recalling clearly how, feeling a bit of HER accidentally under my hoof, I'd immediately lifted it off again. SHE sat up, to my relief, and got to HER feet, coming over to pick up my trailing reins and remove my bridle. My companion stood guard in that silly protective way she has.

'You've hurt HER with your bad manners, barging past HER!"

SHE scratched my companion's poll and gave her a treat - rightfully mine - and toddled off. OK, SHE did offer me a treat, but my companion suggested it'd be better if I allowed her this extra.

I've been quite miserable this afternoon, as my companion has read the Riot Act, reminding me of our code, which says that though we're stronger than two-legs, they rule us, and can make things very unpleasant if we don't co-operate. Furthermore, I've had it impressed on me (with a painful nip into the bargain) that SHE is an extremely kind two-leg, worth keeping. OK, I get it. I'm in the naughty corner.

24. "Smile for the camera!"

"Smile for the camera, Picasso!" SHE coaxed.

SHE's done a great deal of coaxing today, I can report. To begin with, having dressed me like a wimp in travel boots and tail protector, HER first challenge was to coax me into that mobile stable, which I haven't seen for two winter coats-worth. I was extremely reluctant, but graciously agreed to accompany my feed bucket up and inside. There followed a bit of travel – I will give HER credit, in that SHE doesn't throw me around, probably because SHE drives it as slowly as everything else SHE does. Next, SHE offloaded me at somewhere I've visited before. Could scent lots of our kind around. Bit of footering from HER, getting my reins in a fankle, before a pair of very businesslike two-legs (Diane and Stephen) on one each side, sorted me out in a most un-SHE-like manner. In fact, one of them actually asserted that I needed to have more manners on the ground! SHE treacherously bleated assent, which impelled me to do a little 'mount me if you dare' dance. SHE almost parted company with me as a result, and I could sense growing antipathy from the other two-legs, but as SHE didn't fall off, I stood in temporary stillness, while they tightened my girths.

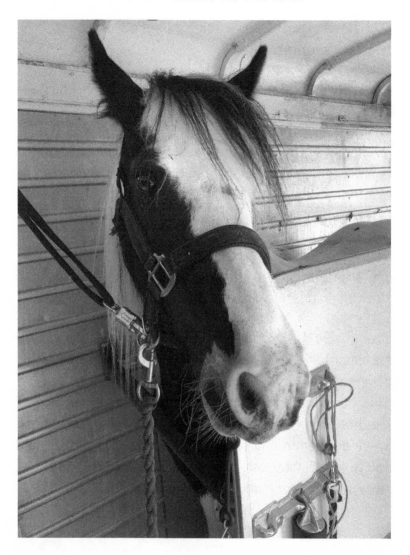

I shan't bore you, though, boy, was I bored by what happened next. To summarise, walking, trotting - far too much trotting - circles, etc. Put in a couple of bucks - nothing serious - to enliven the proceedings, but disappointingly, SHE stayed put, and actually legged me on.

"I'd have used that stick!" hollered Stephen, the two-leg-in-chief.

Hah! SHE knows and I know and we both know we both know where that would go...

"Hello!" I offered to the bigger boy, also condemned to walk and trot around with me. He merely rolled an eye in my direction, before turning away in hopeless serfdom.

Stephen correctly assessed that I am a Character, and that I ought to do well in-hand. The only in-hand that interests me, is a snack.

Everything passes, and having lavishly decorated my transport with poop, we finally arrived back home, my companion whinnying as one isolated for a decade. SHE coaxed and coaxed me to mosey on down out of the horsebox. Patiently, I looked at HER, and shook my head, reminding HER to untie me, before I could oblige. SHE was contrite, and I stepped gratefully away from my accumulated poop-pile.

25.   My Picasso-perfection

Time's winged chariot has had no detrimental effects whatsoever upon my Picasso-perfection, in all my seasons here. Not a wrinkle, black hair still jet black, white hair as lovely as ever. I gallop gaily up my sprouting spring field bucking gracefully in sheer pleasure at sunshine and fresh grass.

The same, I note, cannot be said of HER.

Biography

Ruth Whittaker is a retired teacher of music and writer, living at the family croft on the east coast of Sutherland, in the Scottish Highlands. Ruth has always loved horses and ponies, acknowledging the irony that although she now has the time and modest wherewithal to indulge her love, she's developed a craven loss of nerve for the livelier aspects of equitation. In consequence, Willows Picasso, that's her full name, a smallish but sturdy piebald mare with two speeds (dead slow, and stop) is probably now Ruth's most suitable mount...if and when Picasso's in the mood for being mounted.

CPSIA information can be obtained
at www.ICGtesting.com
Printed in the USA
BVHW082305301122
653184BV00003B/25